Pro and CONRAD

Pro and ~~Conrad~~

Paul Conrad

NEFF-KANE
San Rafael, California

Published by Neff-Kane
San Rafael, California

ISBN: 0-89141-098-8

Library of Congress Catalog Card Number 79-53874

Book project originated by Don Mastrangelo
Color photographs by Fred Farish and Danny Lehman
Interior book design by Mark Jacobsen
Art direction by Joseph M. Roter
Typesetting by Publications Services of Marin
Printed by Kingsport Press, Kingsport, Tennessee

For Kay
who made this book possible
and our four children
who made it necessary

Contents

Foreword

PAUL CONRAD! The very name strikes fear in the evil hearts of men all over the world. This mild-mannered, fifty-five-year-old sex symbol can suddenly turn into a ferocious tower of rage, jabbing his stiletto pen into the most sensitive areas of pompous behinds.

Wherever there is corruption, greed, lying, or hypocrisy, everyone says, "This is a job for Conrad." Ducking into a telephone booth in the lobby of the *Los Angeles Times,* Conrad strips off his clothes, picks up a drawing pad, and in a matter of minutes creates a cartoon which will bring the guilty parties to the bar of justice to get their just desserts.

Were it not for Conrad, no man, woman, or child would be safe in America today. His trenchant political commentaries, which not only appear in the *Times* but are syndicated in 150 newspapers, are our only protection against men and women who would rob us of our constitutional heritage.

Who is Paul Conrad? Very little is known about him. He was born on the planet Krypton, the son of Marlon Brando and some woman whose name I never got. Raised by a couple on an Iowa farm, Conrad first discovered his amazing drawing powers while attending the University of Iowa. He worked on the *Denver Post* for thirteen years before deciding there was much more evil in California than there was in Colorado.

He couldn't have arrived at a better time. We were involved in a lousy war, our leaders were lying through their teeth, credibility of government had hit a new low, and we finally wound up with a president who said publicly he was not a crook.

During these brutal periods Conrad hardly left his telephone booth. Slashing out at Johnson, Nixon, and Agnew, Conrad did more to defoliate Orange County than all the herbicides in the U.S. Army Chemical Corps.

As readers howled in anger Conrad calmly dropped his cartoon bombs on a disbelieving public. Eventually he was proven right, which didn't stop many of them from still howling.

I don't know Paul Conrad well. I met him only once when I caught him siphoning gas out of my car. But that chance meeting was enough to make me a life-long friend.

As with most editorial cartoonists, Conrad is a soft-spoken man who wouldn't hurt a fly—unless the fly happened to be president of the United States or was thinking of running for office.

Conrad is on almost everyone's enemy list, although that doesn't stop his victims from calling up the morning after he's done a particularly savage job on them, requesting the original which they want to frame in their offices.

He asked me to write this introduction to his book, which of course needs no introduction. If you don't understand what he's trying to say, you're in much more trouble than you think.

As a person who works in the same vineyards, I am an admirer, a long-standing fan, and a colleague who wishes him no harm.

If I have any criticism, it's that Conrad did such a good job on Nixon that none of us have old Dick to kick around anymore.

ART BUCHWALD

Acknowledgments

The author wishes to acknowledge the editorial assistance of Les Guthman and the editorial research of Janet Nippell.

Where have all the leaders gone?

Was it only twelve years between John Kennedy's "Ask not what your country can do for you, rather ask what you can do for your country," and Richard Nixon's "I am not a crook"? Or Jerry Ford's "Trust must be earned," and "The people won't stand for a presidential pardon"?

Jimmy Carter's "Why not the best?"
Good question.

Jerry Brown called for "lowered expectations." While upping his, of course.

When *did* it all start?

The 1964 presidential campaign? With President Johnson talking peace while planning the escalation of U.S. troops in Vietnam to 500,000? Or with the de-escalation of his war on poverty? And finally his announcement that he would not run for re-election.

Next there was Nixon's "secret plan" to end the war, promised in his presidential campaign of 1968. Remember? A bad dream repeating itself. It consisted mainly of continuing the war until the 1972 campaign.

Deception and secrecy were the operational words.

Then Watergate. More deception. More secrecy. Stonewalling. The CIA. The IRS. ITT. "Enemy" lists. In the end, a final irony. The president's resignation after two years of deception, hung by his own tapes.

Followed by eighteen months of Ford's caretaker presidency—ennobled only by the withdrawal of troops from Vietnam. Ignobly, he had finally accomplished Nixon's "peace with honor."

And today, Carter's failure, or inability, to lead. Congressional paralysis. Public lack of confidence in elected officials—local, state and national.

The recent Bicentennial recalled earlier leaders. 1776–1976. Jefferson, Franklin, Adams. They wouldn't have recognized the place.

Where, indeed, have all the leaders gone?

Where Have All the Leaders Gone?

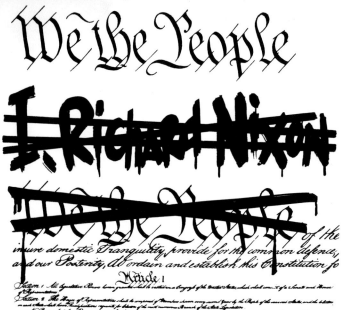

One Flew over the Cuckoo's Nest

THERE ARE SMILES
THAT MAKE YOU HAPPY...

THERE ARE SMILES
THAT MAKE YOU BLUE...

THERE ARE SMILES THAT
FILL YOUR HEART WITH GLADNESS...

OR THAT BORE YOU
THROUGH AND THROUGH...

"Well! I've often seen a cat without a grin," thought Alice; "But a grin without a cat! It's the most curious thing I ever saw!"

The Carter Brothers' Foreign Policy

Carter Proposes Plan to Make It Easier to Fire Inept Federal Employees
— **News Item**

"It's a horse." "Camel." "Steer." "Redwood." "Bummer."

Seven Days in May

Reagan Hood — He takes from the poor and gives to the rich!

"Let's overthrow the government!" "Which government?"

'Eyeball-to-Eyeball'

12

The Men Who Played God

The Hanging Tree

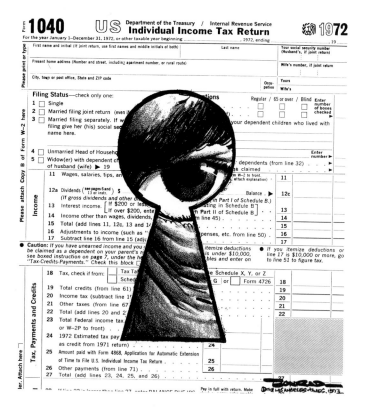

14

The FBI Always Gets Its Man

Rush to Judgment

THE GRAY HOUSE

©THE LOS ANGELES TIMES. 1973

This Is Your FBI

"Don't make waves . . . !"

The Domino Theory

"I've got to go now. . . . I've been appointed Secretary of
Defense and the Secret Service men are here!"

The Sap Is Running in the Maple Trees of New Hampshire

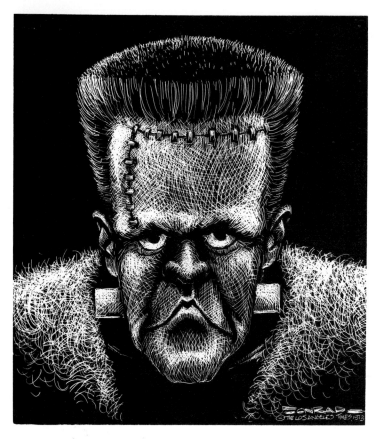

Son of Nixonstein

The King Is Dead. . . . Long Live the Presidency!

22

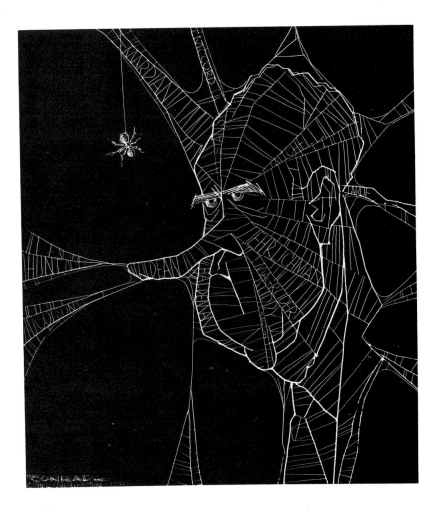

O that I were as great as is my grief, or lesser than my name!
Or that I could forget what I have been,
Or not remember what I must be now!

King Richard II, Act III, Scene III

23

"He says he's from the phone company . . . ."

" . . . Four more weeks! . . . Four more weeks! . . ."

"Oh, nothing much. . . . What's new with you, John?"

"Alas, poor Agnew, Mitchell, Stans, Ehrlichman, Haldeman, Dean, Kalmbach, LaRue, Mardian, Strachan, McCord, Liddy, Chapin, Hunt, Colson, Krogh, Magruder, Young—I knew them . . . ."

CONRAD
© THE LOS ANGELES TIMES. 1977

"How would you like to be introduced . . . ?"

"I'm sorry—I don't recognize any of them . . . !"

The Agony and the Ecstasy

"I gave them a sword."

33

34

All the President's Men — 1975

"As President, Jerry, you could grant me clemency.
. . . But, it would be wrong!"

"Go ye and spend no more."

Turning the Economy Around

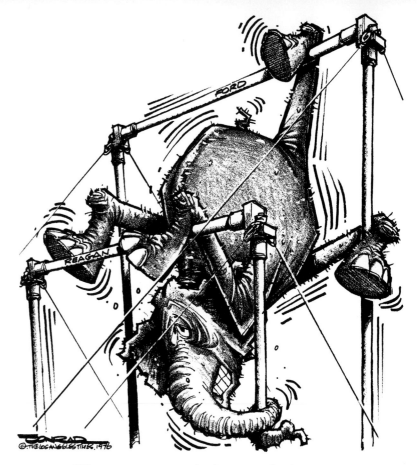

Who were you expecting? . . . Nadia Comaneci?

" . . . Gum . . . ?"

A Reagan-Wallace Ticket

39

First, you get their attention . . . .

The Lemmings

"This is the captain speaking: This is a disaster, but it is also a great opportunity . . . !"

"From the Valley of the Jolly—ho, ho, ho—Green Giant!"

Milk has something for every body

43

'The stockings were hung by the chimney with care,
in hopes that Tongsun Park soon would be there.'

"I gave at the office . . . ."

THERE ARE SOME CROOKED MEN,
WHO WALKED A CROOKED MILE,
AND FOUND A CROOKED SIXPENCE,
AGAINST A CROOKED STILE.

THEY BOUGHT A CROOKED CAT,
WHICH CAUGHT A CROOKED MOUSE,
AND THEY ALL LIVE TOGETHER,
IN A LITTLE CROOKED HOUSE.

"What do you mean—there weren't any throats cut?"

TAIWAN IS THE SOLE GOVERNMENT OF CHINA!

Confusion Says . . . .

"Brother Brown is in conference. . . . Can I help you?"

"It looks like Brother Brown has gone over the wall!"

48

CLOSE TO THE WESTERN SUMMIT THERE IS THE DRIED AND FROZEN CARCASS OF A LEOPARD. NO ONE HAS EXPLAINED WHAT THE LEOPARD WAS SEEKING AT THAT ALTITUDE. —THE SNOWS OF KILIMANJARO

49

"Another fine mess you've gotten us into, Ollie. . . . "

"Ya' know, Bert, Ah never (chew) could figure out
(crunch) why Nixon didn't eat (chomp) those tapes!"

GET A GOOD GRIP ON THAT THUMB, JERRY BROWN... WE'RE TAKING AWAY YOUR SECURITY BLANKET!

$5 BILLION SURPLUS

WITH APOLOGIES TO LINUS

Turning the Other Cheek

An eclipse of this nature will not be seen again in this country in this century.

War and Peace

Vietnam. Or was it Vietnumb?

It all began with 'advisors' sent by Eisenhower. By the time of Kennedy's death, there were 24,000 such 'advisors.'

No one could hear the echo of MacArthur's advice, "Never get into a land war in Asia." Or Eisenhower's "No one could be more bitterly opposed to getting the United States in a hot war in that region than I am."

And, after three administrations, plus 800,000 U.S. troops, there were some other figures: 50,000 dead; 300,000 casualties. Americans. Not to mention millions of Vietnamese, Cambodian, Laotian and North Vietnamese.

The final withdrawal in chaos. The 'body count' finally ended. The war dissolved in bitterness. Refugees. POW's. Grudging amnesty. And the growing realization that the third world was emerging for better and worse.

In the Middle East, the peace efforts have spanned three administrations. And before that, 2,000 years. Political divisions, religious disputes, hatred, jealousy, bloodshed.

As if shuttling between Washington and Harvard, Henry Kissinger went from Tel Aviv to Cairo to Geneva to Jerusalem to Alexandria to Washington— and back again—in search of a formula for peace.

Then the stunning announcement of Anwar Sadat's Christmas visit to Jerusalem heightened hope. Carter's dogged persistence in the Camp David meetings produced the accord signed in 1979 between Israel and Egypt.

A new era? Or a temporary cease-fire? We don't know. The most volatile issues are still to be decided. And yet, the hope of peace in the Middle East has become a reality—for the first time in generations.

'I sing of arms and the man . . .' — Virgil's *Aeneid*

Backing out of the Saloon

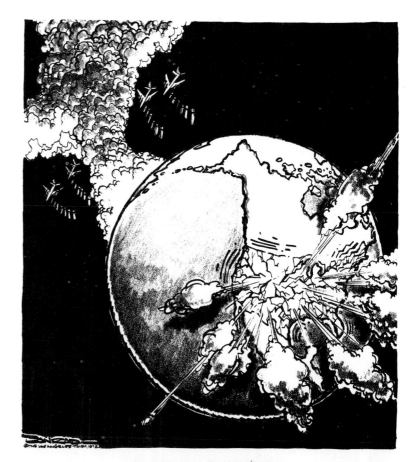

Deep Penetration Bombing

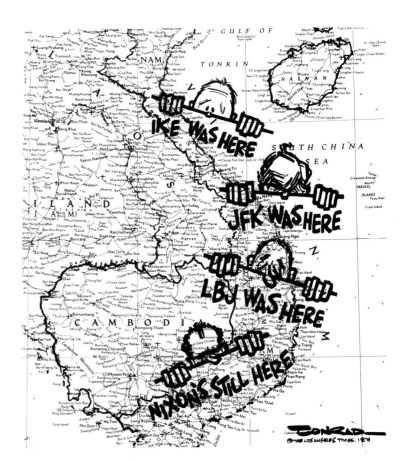

The Nixonization of the War

"If only there'd been a Vietnam moratorium five years ago. . . ."

"Son . . . !" "Dad . . . !"

Dear Mrs. Nixon and Julie:
    I appreciate your offer to give your lives to defend the South Vietnamese. Unfortunately, it comes too late to save my son who . . . . .

But Jesus turning unto them said, "Daughters of Jerusalem, weep not for me, but weep for yourselves and your children."
—St. Luke 23:28

64

"I feel I could be useful to society." —Lt. Calley

The Light at the End of the Tunnel

"... Four more years? ... Four more years? ..."

CAMBODIA WITH $222 MILLION IN U.S. AID

CAMBODIA WITHOUT $222 MILLION IN U.S. AID

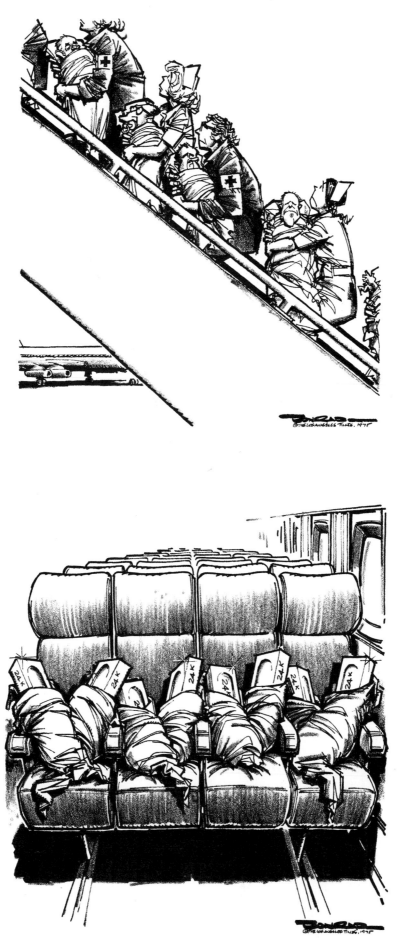

South Vietnam Government Seeks Carrier for Orphans to Switzerland. — News Item

'Victory finds a hundred fathers—Defeat is an orphan.'

Era of Reconciliation

Man on a White Horse

"I was maybe the last Vietnam casualty."

"If the doctor ever prescribes B-1 for you . . . take it . . . !"

Borne Again

I've never seen a purple cow,
I never hope to see one;
But I can tell you, anyhow,
I'd rather see than B-1.

A Star Is Born

AID FOR ANGOLA

AFRICAN QUEEN

CONRAD
FOR THE LOS ANGELES TIMES 1976

A Product of South Africa

78

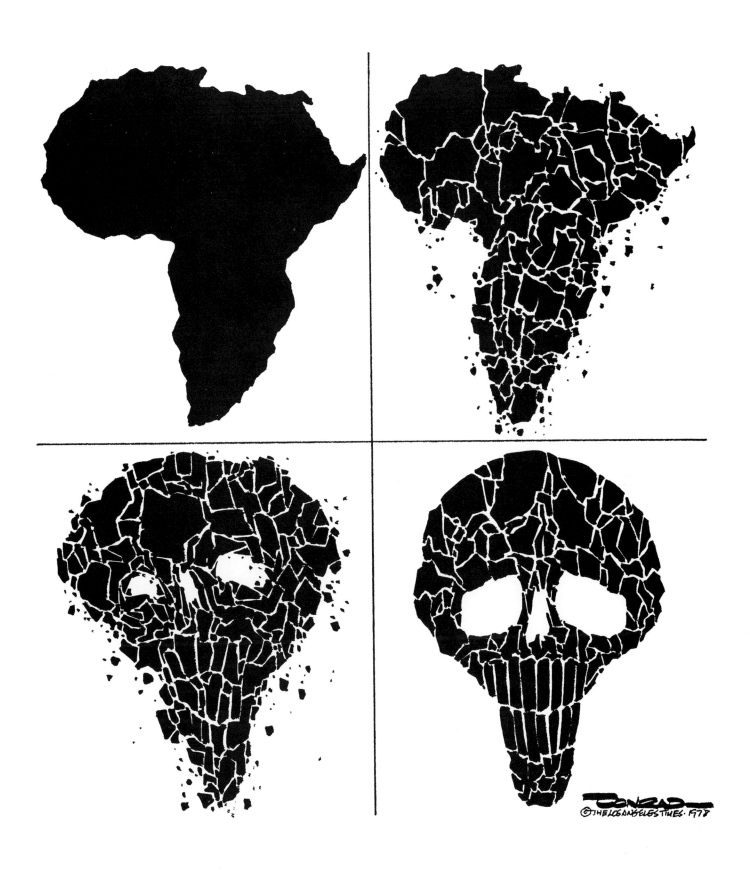

All the World's a Cage

"The opinions expressed do not necessarily represent those
of the sponsor or of management!"

"How many divisions has the Pope?" — Josef Stalin

"To a peaceful and tranquil life for millions . . . !"

. . . and for those who made the 1977 Nobel Peace Prize necessary . . . .

83

Biting the Bullet

A Question of Priorities . . . .

'An eye for an eye; a tooth for a tooth; a life for a life. . . .'

The West Bank as Begin Sees It

A Future Horowitz . . . A Future Einstein . . . A Future Salk . . . .

88

The Eighth Wonder of the World

20th Century Man

The first half of the century was hallmarked by the euphoria of the Twenties—prohibition made notable by speakeasies, bathtub gin, jazz, short skirts and the Charleston. Happy days are here again.

Those times were played out, though, at 78 rpm.

Today, the speed is more like 33⅓ rpm. Or faster. The highs higher, the lows lower.

The euphoria burst, like a balloon, with Black Friday and the crash of '29. Deprived of a non-renewable resource, money.

Today's soaring inflation is the hallmark of the second half of the century. The non-renewable resource, oil. A delicate economy stretched to its breaking limit, its lifeline reaching all the way to the Mideast—and threatened.

There are other problems. Decaying cities, unhealthful air, polluted water. Crime in the streets, and crime in corporate board rooms.

The solutions? Don't look to the government. Growing like some giant malignancy, with bureaucratic fingers reaching ever more into new tender areas, it is unable to cope.

It has become one of the problems. Government's prime response seems to be vast encroachment into individuals' lives, their Constitutional rights and guarantees.

These are the issues that touch us all. But who speaks to the frustrations and outrages of the common man? The cartoonist, for one, with his daily squares of satire, larger than life, more serious than silly.

The cartoonist speaks neither in the realm of propaganda, nor in an attempt to influence. He is simply the voice of the individual, longing to be heard.

Would that everyone had the forum of the editorial cartoonist, or a means of stating one's objections to a multiplicity of annoyances, large or small.

But until that happens, everybody to your window: "I'm mad as hell, and I'm not gonna take it anymore —if I can ever find out who's doing it to me!"

**Another Spaceship Low on Water, Oxygen, and Other Life
Support Systems**

'And on the seventh day he was still waiting for the environmental impact report.'

Two Men Held in Plot to Poison Chicago's Water Supply — News Item

'The time has come,' the walrus said, 'to talk of many things: of crude—and spills—and tanker ships—of oil cartels—and kings.'

"We are holding the Northeast hostage! Deregulate natural gas or they freeze!"

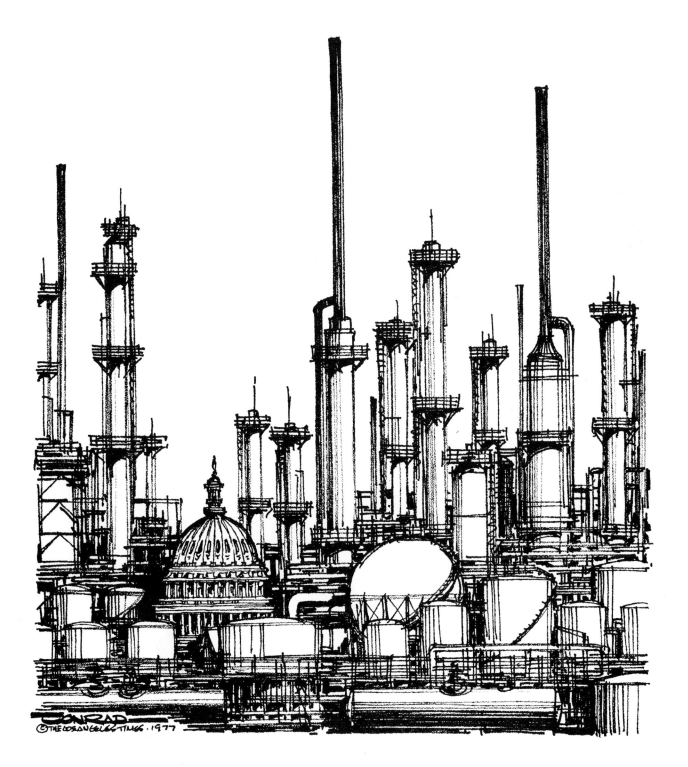

CONRAD
©THE LOS ANGELES TIMES · 1977

"I pledge allegiance to the flag of the country that gives me the best deal. . . . "

OPEC: Oil Producing & Exploiting Companies

"You can trust your car,
To the man who wears the star!"

"You wanta' take away our gusto . . . !?"

The Oilatollah Khompanies

" . . . Decontrol! . . . Decontrol! . . . Decontrol! . . . "

WINDFALL PROFITS

The Bottom Line

110

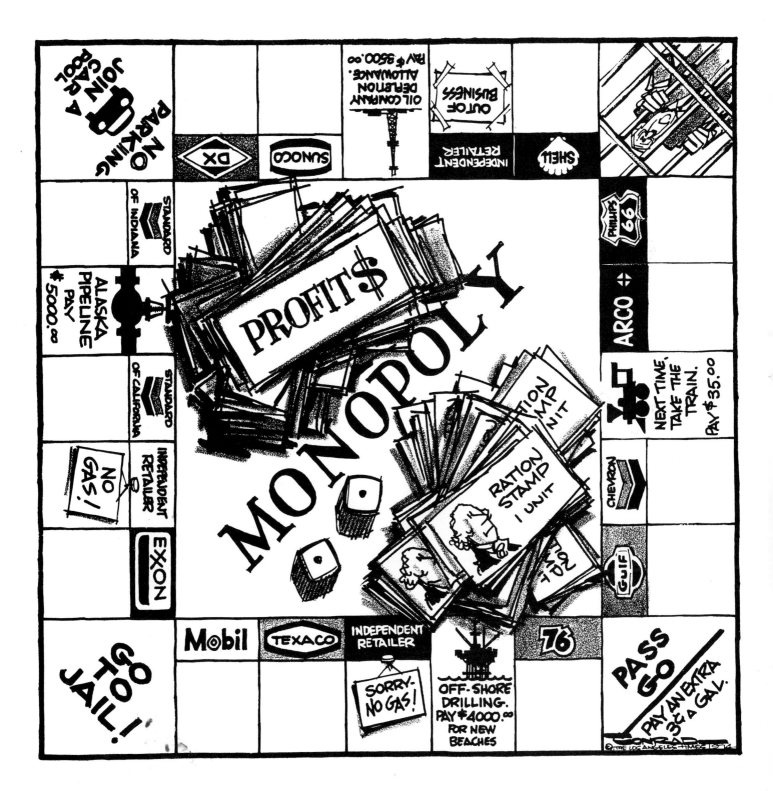

111

"Waiting in those gas lines used to drive me up the wall!"

California Syndrome

"We crack corn and Jimmy don't care,
We crack corn and Jimmy don't care. . . ."

American Gothic — 1970

"Let us give thanks for America's grain harvest . . . ."

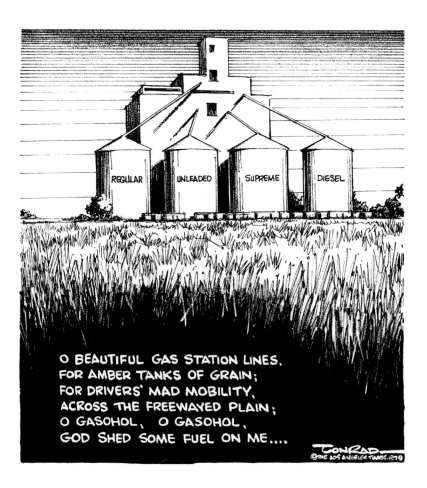

O BEAUTIFUL GAS STATION LINES.
FOR AMBER TANKS OF GRAIN;
FOR DRIVERS' MAD MOBILITY,
ACROSS THE FREEWAYED PLAIN;
O GASOHOL, O GASOHOL,
GOD SHED SOME FUEL ON ME....

Piggyback

Carter's Attack on Inflation

Truth in Advertising

" . . . Blood Pressure? . . . Pulse? . . . BankAmericard?
. . . Master Charge? . . . "

**One out of Every Three Doctors Paid Under Medical Plans
Found Cheating on Income Tax.** — News Item

"This is a stickup . . . ."

Banks' Prime Lending Rate at All-Time High.
—News Item

"It sure is!"

"WE'RE to blame for the riots?! . . . Why, I've never been in a ghetto in my life!"

Black Teenagers 40% Unemployed — News Item

Reflecting Pool

126

Speaking of Child Pornography . . . .

'. . . One nation, divisible, with liberty and justice for some.'

Nothing unusual happened on the way to school again today . . .

Boston's Bicentennial Celebration

" . . . and leave the driving to us!"

"We're low on white . . ."

UNIVERSITY
SAUDI OF
~~SOUTHERN~~ CALIFORNIA

133

"If you don't like it here, why don't you people go back where you came from!"

"No country has ever observed the terms of a treaty if it suited its national purposes to break that treaty."
— **Reagan on the Panama Canal Treaty**

"Thanksgiving . . . That's when you get the turkey and I get the feathers!"

"Like Haldeman, Mitchell and Ehrlichman, I'm sorry and I won't let it happen again!"

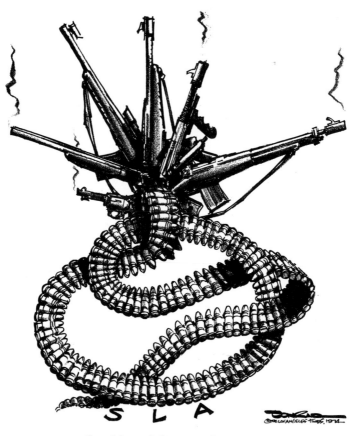

Speaking of Overreaction . . . .

137

'Bless us, O Lord, and these thy gifts which we are about to receive from what is left of our Social Security check. ...'

A society is judged by the way it cares for its youth and its aged.

139

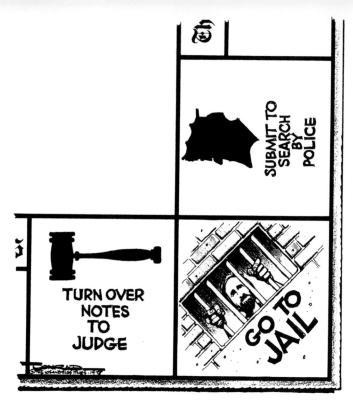

The Newspaper Game

" . . . Copy Boy . . . !"

Vatican Prohibits Ordination of Women as Priests Because Christ's Representatives Must Have a 'Natural Resemblance' to Him.
—News Item

"Joan, you still have time to recant!"

"Sexism, Hell! We did the same thing to Earl Warren!"

Question: Which of these vehicles has more bolts holding its engine on?

It's not nice to fool Mother Nature!

"You people are nothing but functional illiterates anyway!"

"To whom it may concern: Our something-or-other, who art in somewhere-or-other, hallowed be thy what-cha-ma-call-it . . ."

147

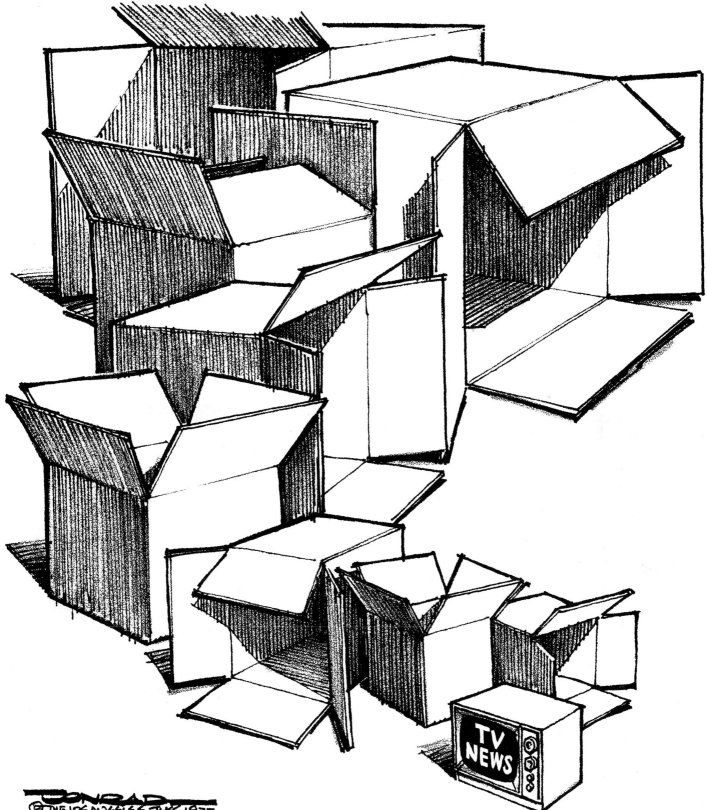

CONRAD
© THE LOS ANGELES TIMES 1977

ME

the People of the United Sta...

insure domestic Tranquility, provide for the common defence, promote the gene
and our Posterity, do ordain and establish this Constitution for the United Sta...

PROPOSITION 13

CONRAD
© THE LOS ANGELES TIMES. 1978

Speaking of American Cults . . .

the living and the dead

Like the three Fates of Virgil's *Aeneid,* Life, Life's Span, and Death, this chapter is a trilogy. But the fates themselves have been replaced with medical decisions, judicial fiat, and social expediency.

Life. Human life.

How can anyone be *against* capital punishment and *for* abortion? Many liberals do not accept that position on abortion. But how can a liberal take any other position than the defense of human life?

The cartoons here deal with these issues. For some, they will be offensive. So be it. A cartoonist can only draw what he believes in good conscience to be correct—consistent with values built up over a lifetime.

The third Fate, Death, is also represented.

Like funerals, obituary cartoons are for the living. A remembrance, a tribute, a statement.

Some even irreverent.

But isn't that what editorial cartooning is all about?

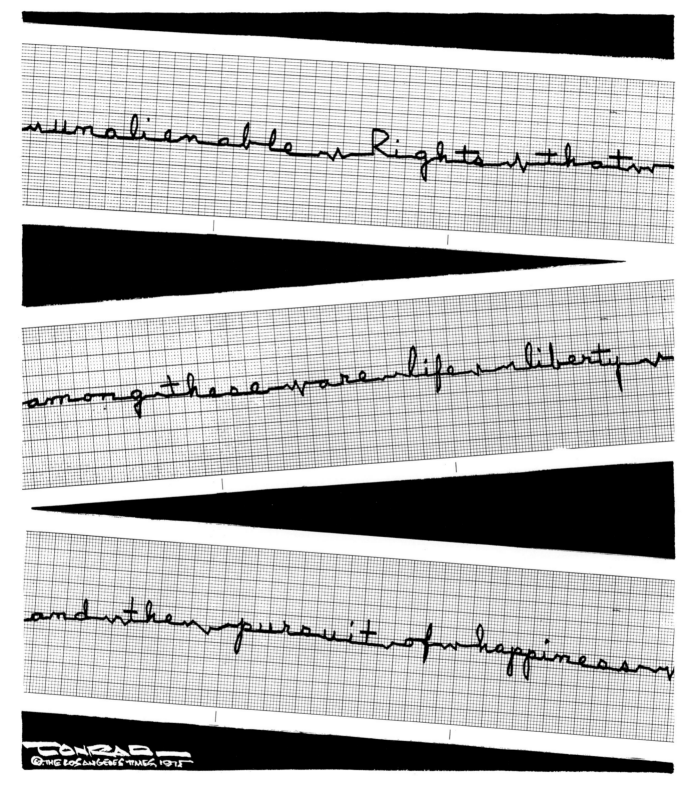

Heartbeat of an Unborn Child

The Butcher's Thumb

Speaking of processes that 'degrade and dehumanize' . . . .

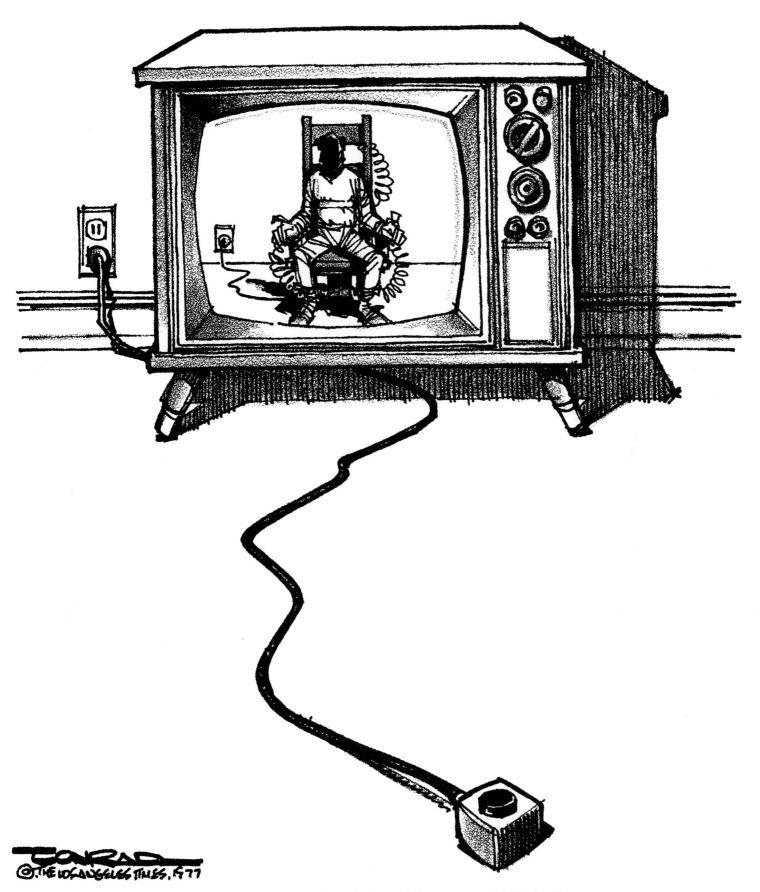

If you are in favor of capital punishment, push this button.

Human Rites

"All I kill are babies!"

"Forgive them, Father, for they know not what they do . . ."

The Way We Were

"You'd better look at what I've got on him!"

" . . . you have the right to remain silent . . . "

And the first shall be last and the last first.

"Goodbye, Grandpa." "Goodbye, Grandpa."
"Goodbye, Grandpa."

"At last! . . . Disneyland!"

"I would never join a club that would accept me as a member."

Douglas

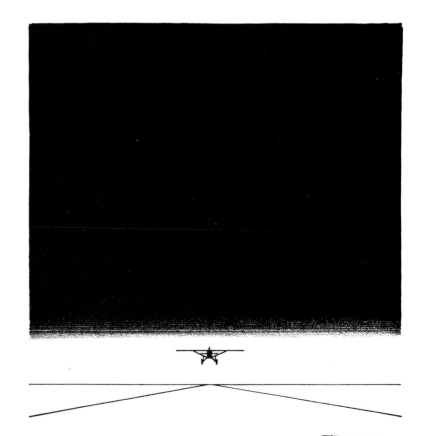

The Spirit of Charles Lindbergh

166

DEATH DEFEATS TRUMAN

The Long March

I Arose a Mother in Israel — Judges V:7

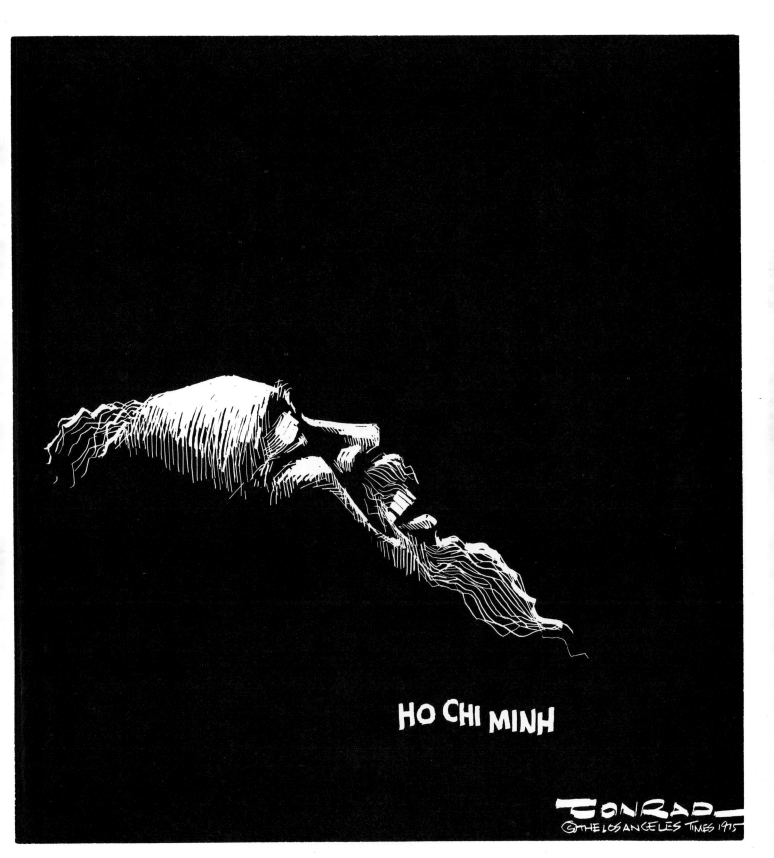

HO CHI MINH

CONRAD
©THE LOS ANGELES TIMES 1975

'Our long national nightmare is over . . . '

Whitney Young—Bridge Builder

We the People

"Would you autograph this for me, Jackie?"

Duke Ellington, 1899–1974

Did You Ever Swing on a Star . . . .

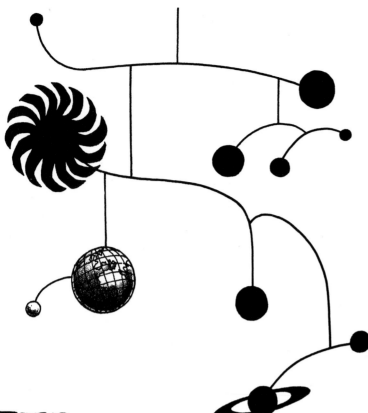

Alexander Calder, 1898–1976

"You know, I never looked at it that way before!"

May God Show His Face to Thee . . . .

Helen Keller, 1880–1968

Satire in Bronze

"I don't know anything about art, but I know what I like."

To many viewing editorial cartoons, "And what I don't like" might well be added.

Editorial cartoons are statements of opinion. They are also line drawings done under a daily deadline and refer generally to current news, both social and political.

This segment consists of cartoons in bronze of individuals. In many cases the personalities have become the embodiment of the issues themselves. They combine the art of cartooning and caricature with the art of sculpture.

But, "is it art?" That might be a good subject for an editorial cartoon. Or another bronze.

RICHARD NIXON
1978/BRONZE/19¾″

JERRY BROWN
1978/BRONZE/9½"

RONALD REAGAN
1978/BRONZE/18⁵/₈″

JIMMY CARTER
1978/BRONZE/19¾"

186

HOWARD JARVIS
1979/BRONZE/12½"

GOLDA MEIR
1979/BRONZE/14¼"

ANWAR SADAT
1979/BRONZE/6¾"

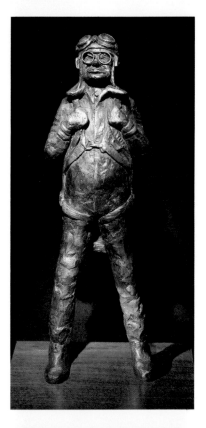

BARRY GOLDWATER
1979/BRONZE/16⅛″

190

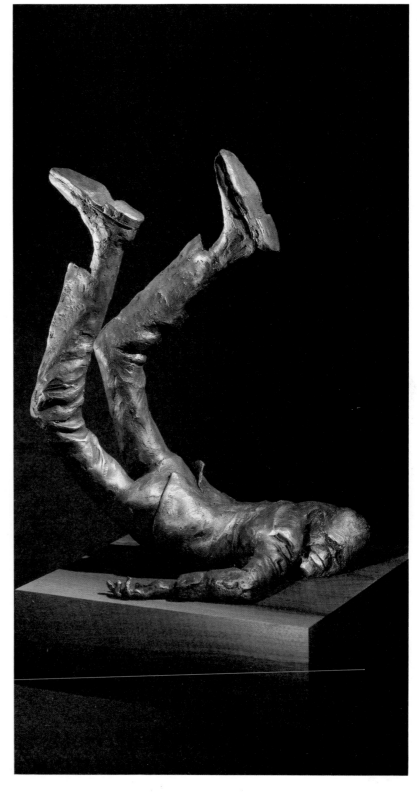

GERALD FORD
1978/BRONZE/11¾″

JOHN KENNEDY
1979/BRONZE/15$^{11}/_{32}$″

192

List of Cartoons

List of Cartoons

20th Century Man

The Living and the Dead